DINOSAUR ADVENTURE Activity Book

Illustrated by Jen Alliston

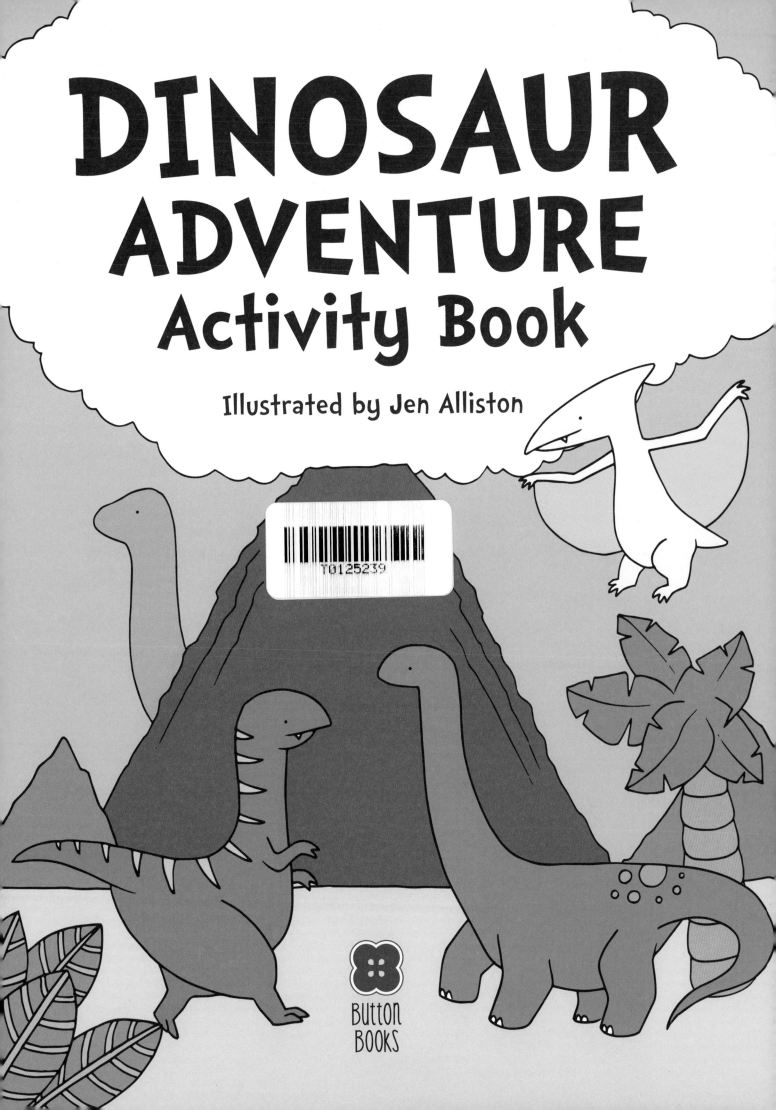

Button BOOKS

Millions and millions of years ago, huge
dinosaurs roamed our planet. Are you ready
to take a trip back into their exciting
world? In this book you'll find loads
of puzzles, mazes, things to make,
coloring, stickers, and games.
Get ready for some dinormous fun!

Meet the dinosaurs

Can you work out which of these dinosaurs match the descriptions below?

Stegosaurus
Slow and steady, this four-legged plant-eater had bony plates down its back. It used its strong tail to fend off predators.

Tyrannosaurus
This big meat-eater moved around on two legs and had strong jaws that could crunch through bone.

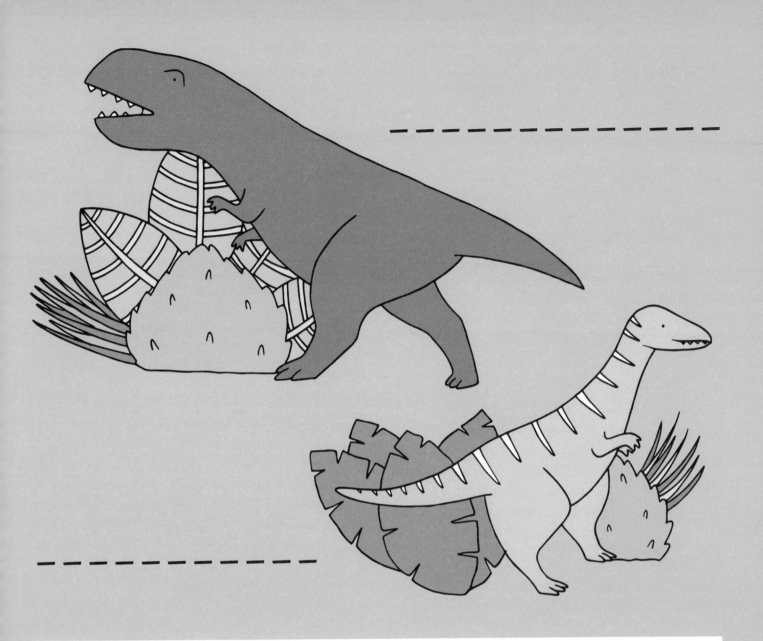

Diplodocus
This four-legged vegetarian had a long neck so that it was able to eat tasty leaves at the top of trees.

Coelophysis
This small meat-eater was fast on its two legs. It would catch small reptiles and insects with its sharp teeth and claws.

Triceratops
This four-legged plant-eater had three horns on its head that it used to defend itself from predators.

Twin bones

Match the pairs of dinosaur bones and color them in.

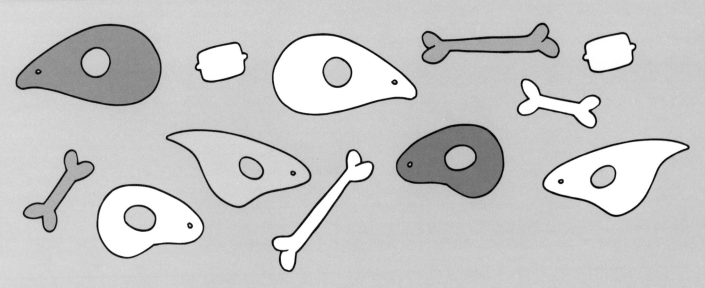

Long story

Do the math problems and see if you can work out which of these dinosaurs was shorter than a London bus.

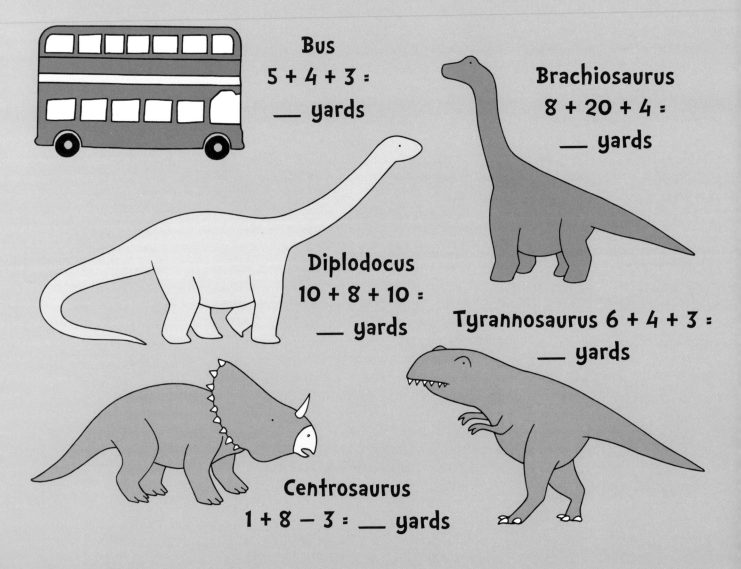

Bus
5 + 4 + 3 =
___ yards

Brachiosaurus
8 + 20 + 4 =
___ yards

Diplodocus
10 + 8 + 10 =
___ yards

Tyrannosaurus 6 + 4 + 3 =
___ yards

Centrosaurus
1 + 8 − 3 = ___ yards

Disappearing act

Complete the fossils to preserve the dinosaur skeletons, then give them names.

Mystery case

Someone who hunts for fossils is called a paleontologist. Can you work out what this one has forgotten to pack?

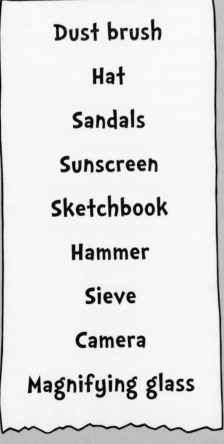

Dust brush

Hat

Sandals

Sunscreen

Sketchbook

Hammer

Sieve

Camera

Magnifying glass

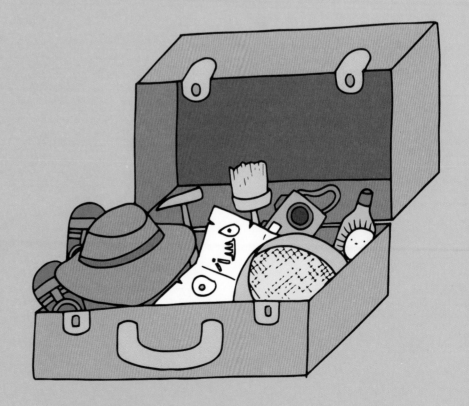

Egg hunt

This dinosaur has lost her egg! Can you help her through the maze to find it?

Dinosaur playmate

One of these dinosaurs wants to play a game. It has four legs, a tail, a horn, and seven spikes on its back. Which one is it?

Back to the bones

Can you work out which skeleton belongs to which dinosaur? Once you have, color them all in.

Animal impostors

Dinosaurs lived in the Mesozoic Era, between 230 and 65 million years ago. Many animals we know today weren't around then. Can you spot the modern imposters in this picture?

Veggie dino

The Brachiosaurus was one of the largest dinosaurs. It could grow to 32 yards in length and ate leaves from the top of trees. Color in this gigantic creature!

Draw a volcano

Volcanoes were very active when dinosaurs were around. Here's how to draw one.

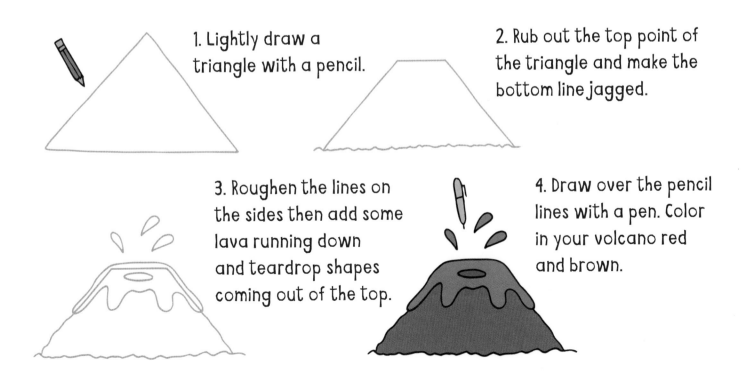

1. Lightly draw a triangle with a pencil.

2. Rub out the top point of the triangle and make the bottom line jagged.

3. Roughen the lines on the sides then add some lava running down and teardrop shapes coming out of the top.

4. Draw over the pencil lines with a pen. Color in your volcano red and brown.

Dotty dinosaur families

Dinosaurs belong to different groups. Follow the numbers to join the dots to see what these different kinds of dinosaurs looked like.

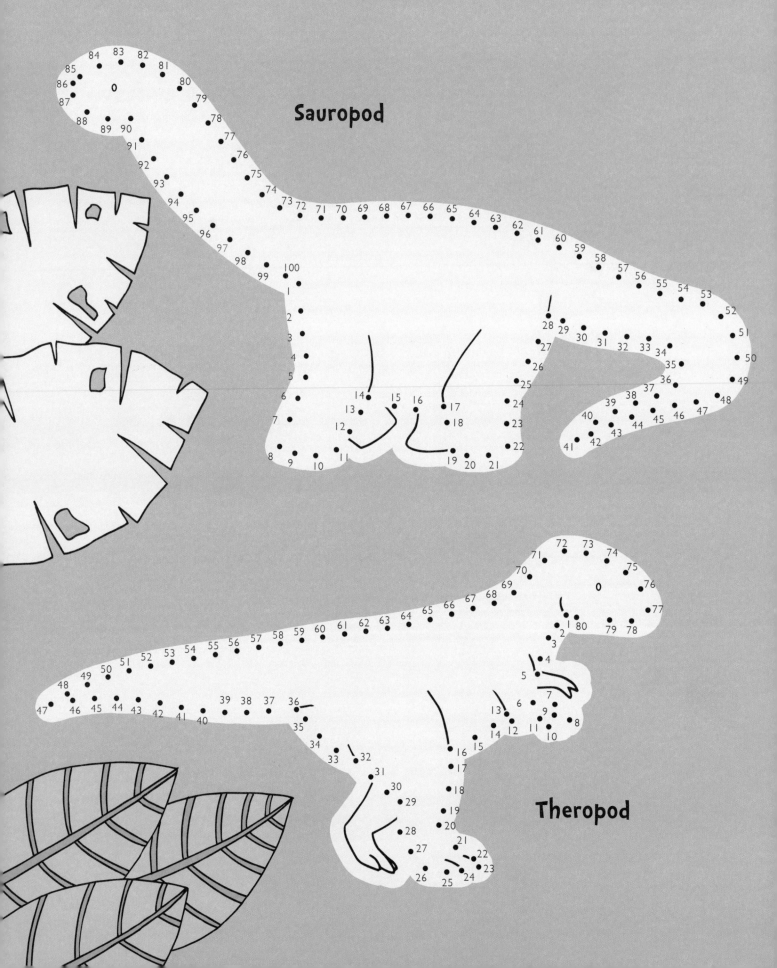

Sauropod

Theropod

Ornithomimosaur

Ceratopsian

Ankylosaurid

13

Jungle jumble

These prehistoric plants look the same, but one is different.
Can you spot the odd one out?

Munch mission

These dinosaurs are hungry. Follow the lines to see what they would like to eat.

Hidey holes

How many dinosaurs can you find hidden in this underwater scene?

Create your own dino

Draw heads, legs, tails, and spikes onto these blobs to turn them into dinosaurs.

Digging for words

Can you find these words related to fossil hunting?

ROCK

CAVE

DINOSAUR

FOSSIL

EXCAVATION

BONES

EXTINCT

J F Y S B V F G N S H D J S E M
X H C A V E Q P L M V P W R X K
K W R Q Y V C S M K L R V F C J
P Q W D F C G B X Z P K Y M A H
D I N O S A U R P Y R Q X C V J
K H P B X Z P X P M V J W R A K
T G B Q S P M V P Q W B K R T P
P R D Q W X C R P L P O K J I F
R F E X T I N C T Q X N P H O S
O Y W Q P K M V X Z Y E G R N F
C D Y P K G D W F O S S I L T W
K P T H K J L M B V Z Q P W X Z

Make your own volcano

You'll need:

Gravel, small stones, sand, or earth

Paper cup

Red food coloring

1 tsp dishwashing liquid

Water

8 fl oz vinegar

¾ tbsp baking soda

Mini toy dinosaurs

1. In your garden make a large mound of gravel, sand, or earth. Place the dinosaurs around the sides.

2. Push the paper cup down into the top of the mound so the rim is level with the top.

3. Fill the cup two-thirds full of water then add the baking soda, dishwashing liquid, and food coloring.

4. Give all the ingredients a good stir.

5. Add the vinegar and watch the lava flow down the volcano! Did your dinosaurs survive?

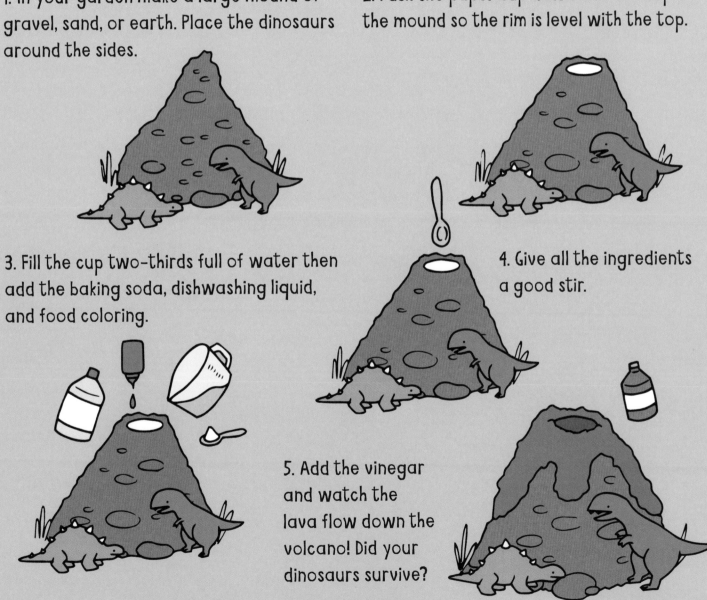

17

Prehistoric chums

There were lots of other creatures around when dinosaurs were on the planet. Using these descriptions, can you label them?

Archaeopteryx
One of the earliest birds, this creature had feathers as well as teeth and a long tail.

Dragonflies
Millions of years before the dinosaurs arrived, these insects were already buzzing around on Earth.

Ichthyosaur
This "fish lizard" looked similar to today's dolphins.

Pterosaur
This flying reptile had large wings made of skin and muscle.

Plesiosaurus
This large reptile lived in the sea and had a short tail and long neck.

Megazostrodon
This small, ratlike animal is thought to be one of the first mammals.

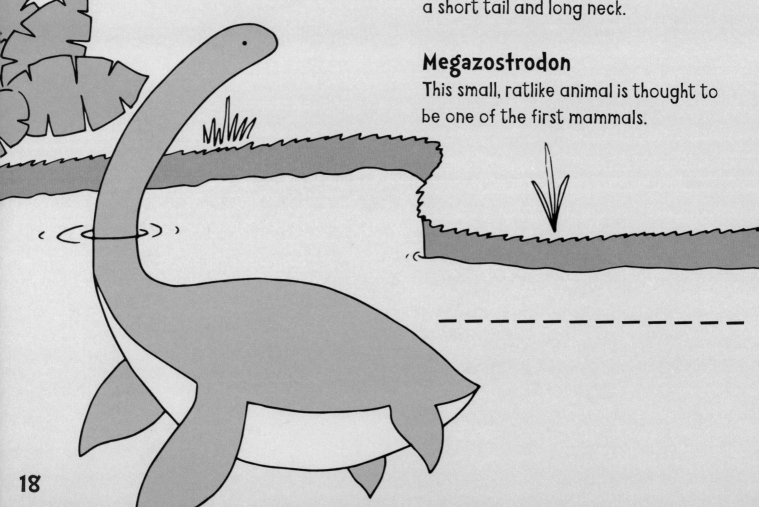

19

Jungle path

Match the dinosaurs to their eggs. Then draw a line through the forest to connect them without touching any palm trees.

Create your own fossil-hunt story

Choose words from the sticker pages to finish this fossil-hunting adventure.

Professor Bones was leading an expedition to find some fossils. Digging with her

[   ], she hit a hard object. Excitedly she called to her fellow

[   ]. "I think we might have found a [   ],"

she said. Quickly they dug deeper and found what looked like an [   ]

bone. But just as they started to [   ], Ned the dog leapt into the

[   ] and dug it up for them! "Wait a minute," said Professor Bones.

"That isn't a [   ] bone, it's from Ned's dinner!"

Make your own dinosaur garden

You'll need:

Ask a grown-up to help!

Pebbles

Toy dinosaurs

Sand

Seashells

Trowel

One large plant pot filled with soil

Clean yogurt container

Small plants such as mini ferns or succulents

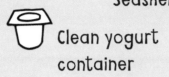

1. Using a trowel, dig small holes into the soil and carefully push in your plants.

2. Dig a bigger hole for the yogurt container, then fill it with water to create a drinking hole.

3. Arrange the pebbles, sand, and seashells.

4. Invite some mini dinosaurs to play!

Prehistoric adventure

Use stickers to add some dinosaur fun to this picture.

Jungle egg count

How many red eggs can you find hidden
in the jungle? And how many blue ones?
How many are there in total?

Mirror image

Draw the missing halves of these dinosaurs and color them to match.

Finders keepers

Can you spot the five differences between these two fossil-hunting pictures?

Counting relics

Write down how many of each fossil you can see.

Crunch bunch

These dinosaurs are hungry! Use the translator to find out what they want to eat.

26

Tall order

Can you put these dinosaurs in height order? Number them from 1 for the smallest to 4 for the tallest, then color them in.

Dinosaurs' footsteps

Follow the footprints to find out whose home is whose.
Then color the front door to match its owner.

Monster market

Color in these shopping dinosaurs. How many eggs can you count?

Dino quarrel

Can you spot the five differences between these two scenes of squabbling dinosaurs?

Supper time

Which Brachiosaurus will reach the tree
to eat its leaves?

Buried bones

Which hole should the paleontologist keep digging to find the fossil?

A   B   C

Dinosaur pairs

How many different dino twins can you spot?
Color them to match.

Getting warmer

Do these math problems to find out which volcano is the most powerful. Color in the one
with the highest number red, the next one orange, and the lowest one yellow.

9 + 8 + 1 = __   2 + 9 + 6 = __   3 + 5 + 4 = __

Spare parts

These poor dinosaurs need your help! Make them complete by adding stickers to give them legs, heads, tails, and spikes.

paleontologists

excavate

fossil

horn

pit

Diplodocus

trowel

spoon

digging

Stegosaurus

enormous

dinosaur

Make your own dinosaur feet

You'll need:

Ask a grown-up to help!

Two empty tissue boxes

Colored paper

Scissors

White paper

Glue stick

Pencil

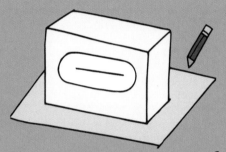

1. Put a tissue box on its side on top of your colored paper and draw round it. Do this for all sides of both boxes. Lastly draw round the top of the box twice.

2. Cut all the pieces out so you have two pieces for the top, four pieces for the long sides, and four pieces for the short sides.

x 4   x 4   x 2

3. Cut a large X in the middle of the two top pieces for your feet to fit through.

4. Stick the top pieces of paper in position on each box.

5. Glue the side pieces to the sides of the boxes.

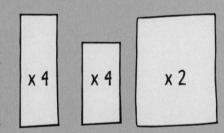

6. Cut out six white triangles to make your dinosaur claws and glue them to the bottom of one of the short edges of each box. Now wear them!

Jurassic landscape

Add some stickers to bring this dinosaur world to life.

Cave dash

Help this dinosaur find her way back to her cave. Don't forget to pick up her egg on the way!

Spiral shapes

Ammonites existed at the same time as dinosaurs and lived in the sea. Lots of fossils have been found. Count how many sections these ones have, then color them in.

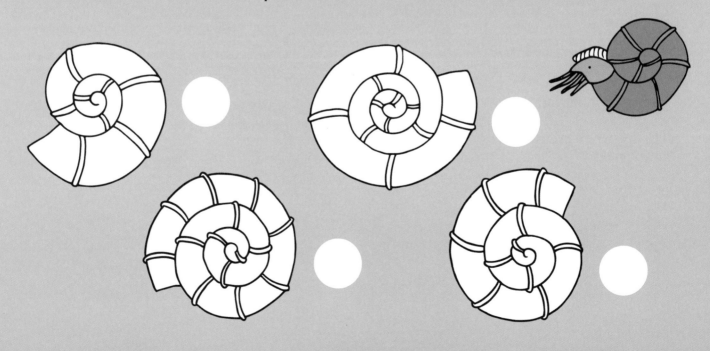

Dinosaur timelines

Different types of dinosaur lived at different times. Follow the trails to find out which dinosaur lived during which period.

Diplodocus

Triceratops

Plateosaurus

Triassic

Jurassic

Cretaceous

Greedy dinosaur

Which dinosaur ate all the tasty ferns? It has two arms, two legs, two horns, and a short tail. Work out who did it and color them all in.

Shadow play

Can you match the dinosaur shadows to the colored ones?

Hide and seek

How many dinosaurs can you find hidden in the jungle?
Color the picture when you have found them.

Make no bones about it

These paleontologists have been digging for hours but haven't found any dinosaur fossils yet. Can you spot the five bones they've missed?

Recycled letters

Can you complete these words, using all the letters in the word DINOSAUR?

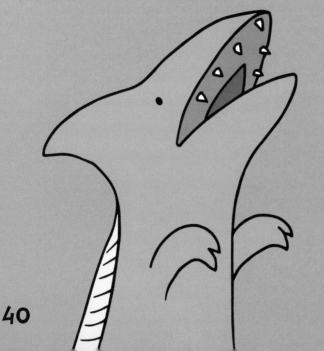

FO_SIL

TRI_SSIC

EXT_NCT

JU_GLE

B_NES

ROA_

J_RASSIC

DIPLO_OCUS

Hatch countdown

Do these math problems to work out which dinosaur egg will hatch first. The dinosaur in the egg with the lowest number will appear first. Now color them all in.

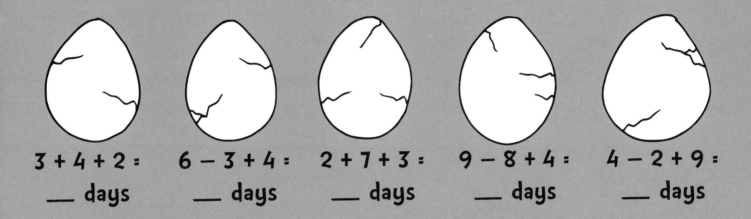

3 + 4 + 2 =
___ days

6 − 3 + 4 =
___ days

2 + 7 + 3 =
___ days

9 − 8 + 4 =
___ days

4 − 2 + 9 =
___ days

Spot the dinosaur

How many spots can you count on this dinosaur? Color all the spots with lots of different colors.

Make a dinosaur mask

You'll need:

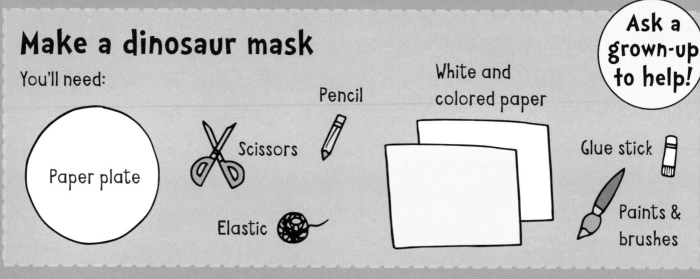

Paper plate

Scissors

Pencil

Elastic

White and colored paper

Glue stick

Paints & brushes

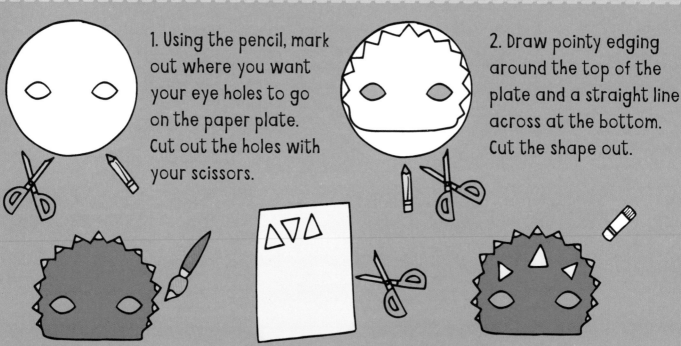

1. Using the pencil, mark out where you want your eye holes to go on the paper plate. Cut out the holes with your scissors.

2. Draw pointy edging around the top of the plate and a straight line across at the bottom. Cut the shape out.

3. Paint your mask whatever color you like.

4. Cut some triangles out of the colored paper.

5. Stick these horns on your dinosaur's forehead.

6. Cut some triangles out of white paper.

7. Glue these on the back of your mask, along the bottom edge, to make teeth.

8. Make holes in the sides with a pencil. Thread the elastic through and secure with a knot. Now wear your mask!

Baby dino nap time

This baby dinosaur is ready for his nap. Help him get back to his nest.

Weighty issues

Work out these problems to find out how heavy these dinos were. Who was the heaviest?

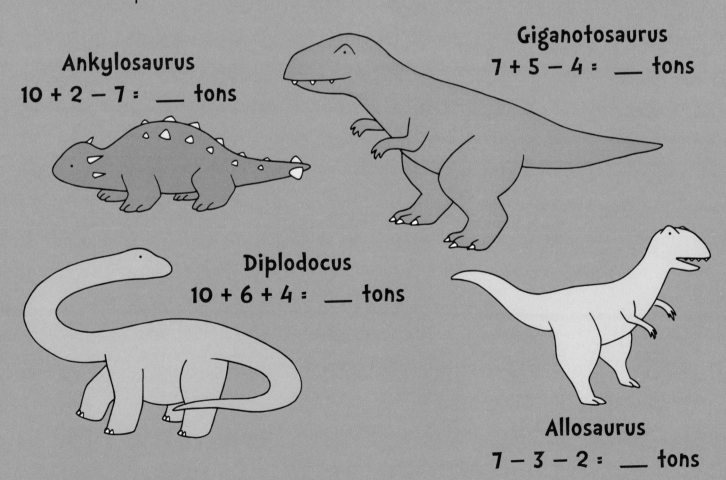

Ankylosaurus
10 + 2 − 7 = __ tons

Giganotosaurus
7 + 5 − 4 = __ tons

Diplodocus
10 + 6 + 4 = __ tons

Allosaurus
7 − 3 − 2 = __ tons

Chew it over

Can you figure out which dinosaur has chomped which leaf?

Hidden dinosaurs

Can you find these dinosaur words?

JURASSIC

FOSSIL

CRETACEOUS

BONES

STEGOSAURUS

DIPLODOCUS

```
P G B J U R A S S I C V K P
T R X H Q P K M Q X R X D Y
G B O N E S W P Z V E V Q P
H X S Y X T P V Y Q T Y X T
K F Q W S E G K J W A P T D
P O R X Z G T Y Q F C Q Y I
W S Z Q V O X C X W E D X P
Q S X D M S C Q V Z O X P L
R I V Q X A F V X Y U Z Q O
V L P V Q U X P Z S D S A H D
Z Y X Q X R W Y X Z V Q L O
X G P Z Y U X P Q F X K C
H Q X A X S W Z S P Y Q F U
D X G X Q Y K Q P W Z Q X S
```

Creepy crawlies

There were lots of insects in prehistoric times. How many of each kind can you spot?

Dotty dino

Join the dots to complete this scary Tyrannosaurus.

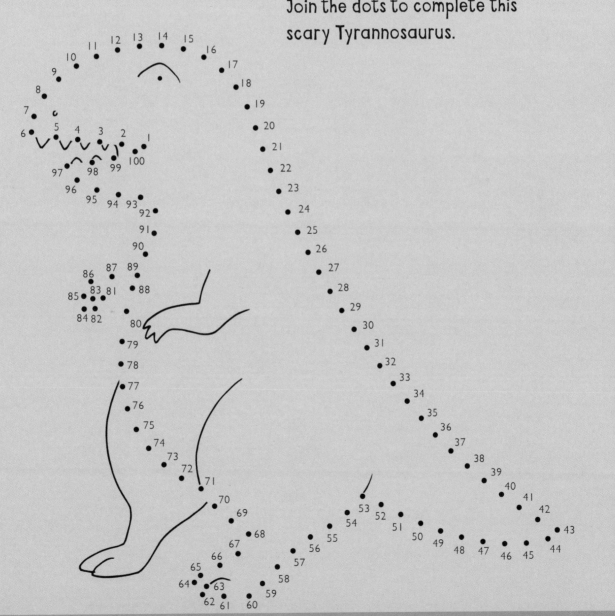

Big city giants

If dinosaurs existed today they might go to visit a big city. Find the dinosaurs' faces on the sticker pages and add them to the right bodies. Then color the city in.

Dotty Steggy

Join the dots to complete this Stegosaurus.

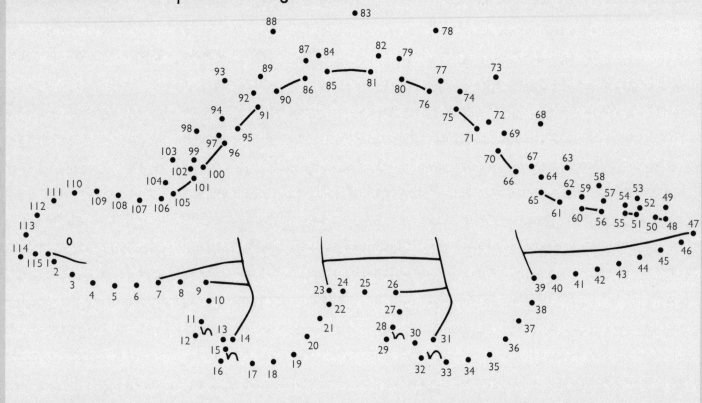

Jurassic jokes

Q: What do you call a dinosaur with dark glasses?
A: Doyouthinkhesaurus

Q: What do you call a sleeping dinosaur?
A: A dino-snore

Q: What is it called when dinosaurs crash into each other?
A: Tyrannosaurus wrecks

Q: What is it called when a dinosaur gets a goal?
A: A dino-score

Make a waffleasaurus

You'll need:

Round waffle

Pineapple ring

Chocolate candy melt

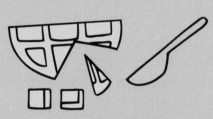
Cookie

Raisin

Knife

1. Cut the waffle in half. One half will be your waffleasaurus's body.

2. Cut out a small triangle from the other half of the waffle to create a tail and two oblongs for legs.

3. Put the body piece of waffle on a plate and place the cookie at one end for the head. Put the waffle tail at the other end. Add two pieces of waffle on the straight edge to make legs.

4. Cut the pineapple ring into wedges and add them along the curve to create spikes.

5. Add the raisin on top of the cookie to make an eye. Break the chocolate candy melt in half and use it as a mouth. Now add a topping of your choice and eat!

49

Funny bones

Can you spot five differences between these fossils?

Flower power

Water lilies existed when dinosaurs roamed the planet. Follow the key to color in this one.

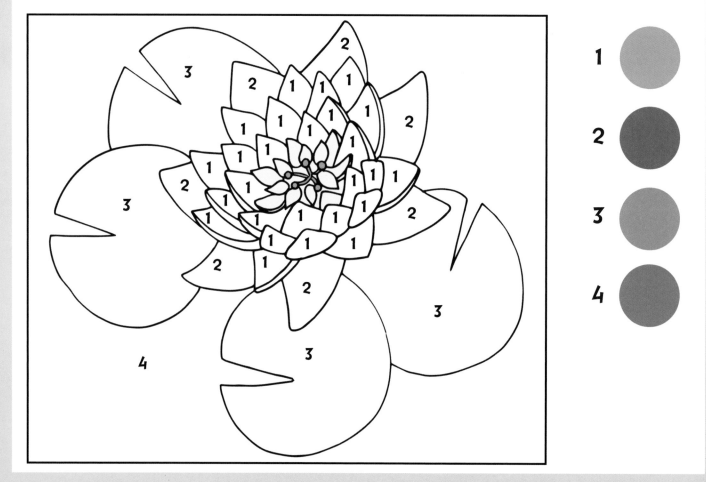

DIY dinosaurs

Use the stickers to complete these dinosaurs.

Make your own dinosaur skeleton

You'll need:

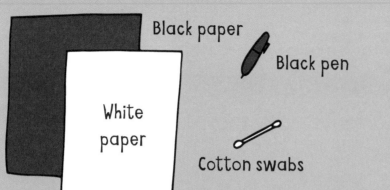

Black paper

 Black pen

Scissors

White paper

Cotton swabs

Pencil

Glue

Ask a grown-up to help!

1. Using this one as a guide, draw a sketch of a Tyrannosaurus skeleton on your black paper.

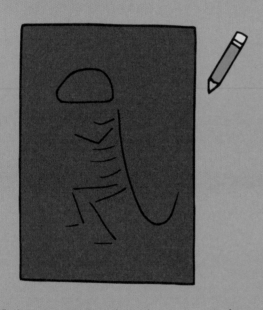

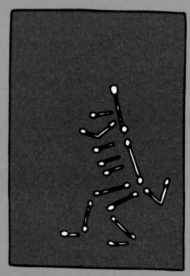

2. Following the drawing, place the cotton swabs on to the sketch so they look like fossil bones. Trim or bend them to fit. Once you're pleased with how it looks, stick the cotton swabs down with glue.

3. Draw and cut out an oval shape for the head, with jagged lines for the teeth.

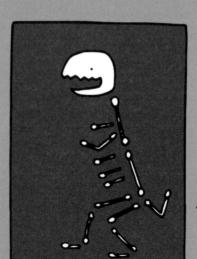

4. Add the skull to your skeleton and glue in place. Color in an eye with the black pen.

Muddled animals

These animals are still around from the dinosaur age. Can you work out what they are?

LETRTU _ _ _ _ _ _

EDCROLICO _ _ _ _ _ _ _ _ _

DRBI _ _ _ _

DRZIAL _ _ _ _ _ _

KENAS _ _ _ _ _

HSRAK _ _ _ _ _

Snake

Shark

Bird

Crocodile

Turtle

Lizard

Fossil race

Which paleontologist will reach the fossil first?

53

Colorful creatures

See how many dinosaurs can you count with:

- Pink spots
- Green tails
- Yellow stripes
- Blue spikes
- Red legs

Jurassic jungle

Cycads are palm-like plants with giant cones that were common in the dinosaur era. Draw the other side of this one, then color it in.

Tasty fact

The word dinosaur comes from the Greek language and means "terrible lizard." Draw a picture of what you think this creature might like to eat.

Walk in the woods

Color these dinosaurs and plants.

Gone missing

Can you work out which dinosaur has lost which egg?

Make your own dinosaur tail

The perfect addition to any outfit—your own dinosaur tail!

Ask a grown-up to help!

You'll need:

Scissors

Ruler

Glue stick

Pencil

Ribbon

Large sheets of dark and light green paper

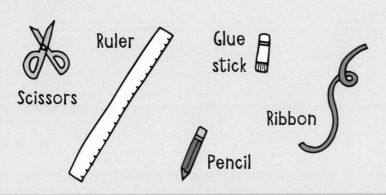

1. Fold the dark green paper in half lengthways. Unfold, then draw a triangle as shown.

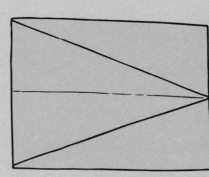

2. Cut your triangle out.

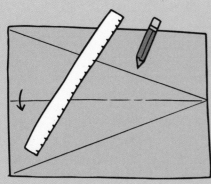

3. Cut out a light green strip that's as long as the longer edge of the triangle and about 3in wide. Cut out some circles too.

4. Fold the strip in a zigzag.

5. Cut one corner off to give you a long strip with a pointed edge when unfolded.

6. Glue your jagged strip along the long edge of the triangle. Glue the other long edge.

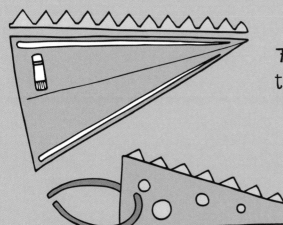

7. Fold and press the edges together to hold the strip.

8. Stick the circles on. Make a hole with the scissors and thread the ribbon through.

9. Tie on and roar!

Meet the dinosaurs (pages 4–5)

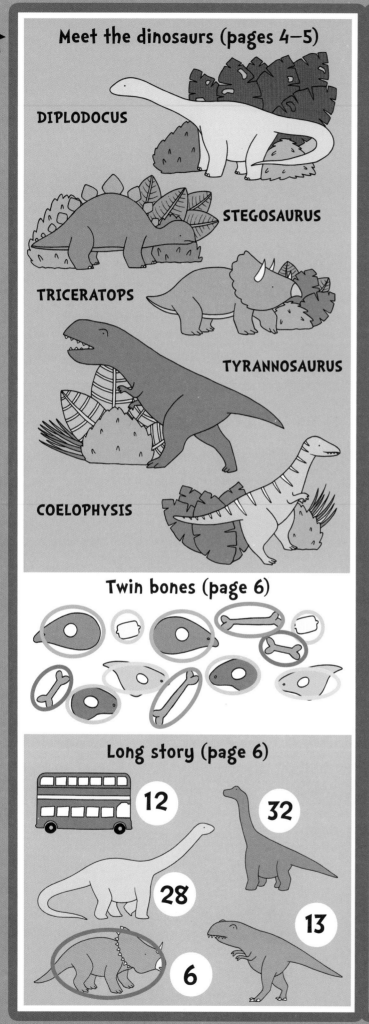

DIPLODOCUS

STEGOSAURUS

TRICERATOPS

TYRANNOSAURUS

COELOPHYSIS

Twin bones (page 6)

Long story (page 6)

12

32

28

13

6

Mystery case (page 7)

The magnifying glass
is missing.

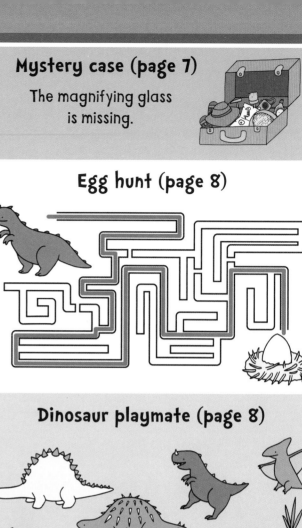

Egg hunt (page 8)

Dinosaur playmate (page 8)

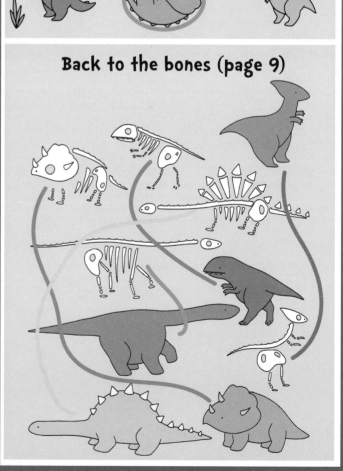

Back to the bones (page 9)

Animal imposters (page 10)

Jungle jumble (page 14)

Munch mission (page 14)

Hidey holes (page 15)

There are 8 dinosaurs.

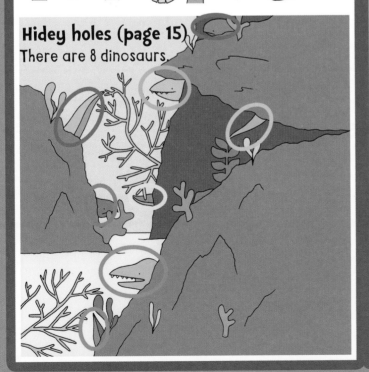

Digging for words (page 16)

J	F	Y	S	B	V	F	G	N	S	H	D	J	S	E	M
X	H	C	A	V	E	Q	P	L	M	V	P	W	R	X	K
K	W	R	Q	Y	V	C	S	M	K	L	R	V	F	C	J
P	Q	W	D	F	C	G	B	X	Z	P	K	Y	M	A	H
D	I	N	O	S	A	U	R	P	Y	R	Q	X	C	V	D
K	H	P	B	X	Z	P	X	M	V	J	W	R	A	K
T	G	B	Q	S	P	M	V	P	Q	W	B	K	R	T	P
P	R	D	Q	W	X	C	R	P	L	P	O	K	J	I	F
R	F	E	X	T	I	N	C	T	Q	X	N	P	H	O	S
O	Y	W	Q	P	K	M	V	X	Z	Y	E	G	R	N	F
C	D	Y	P	K	G	D	W	F	O	S	S	I	L	T	W
K	P	T	H	K	J	L	M	B	V	Z	Q	P	W	X	Z

Prehistoric chums (pages 18–19)

PTEROSAUR

DRAGONFLIES

ARCHAEOPTERYX

MEGAZOSTRODON

PLESIOSAURUS

ICHTHYOSAUR

Jungle path (page 20)

Jungle egg count (page 24)

There are 4 red eggs and 8 blue eggs,
so there are 12 in total.

Finders keepers (page 25)

Counting relics (page 26)

Crunch bunch (page 26)

Tall order (page 27)

Dinosaurs' footsteps (page 27)

Monster market (page 28)

There are 11 eggs.

Dino quarrel (page 28)

Supper time (page 29)

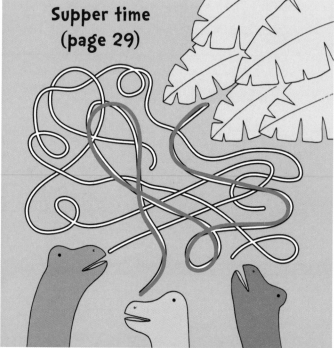

Buried bones (page 30)

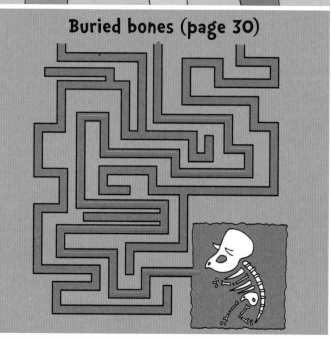

Dino pairs (page 31)
There are 7 pairs.

Getting warmer (page 31)

18   17   12

Cave dash (page 36)

Spiral shapes (page 36)

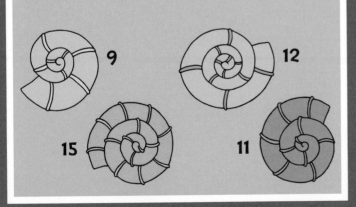

9   12

15   11

Dinosaur timeline (page 37)

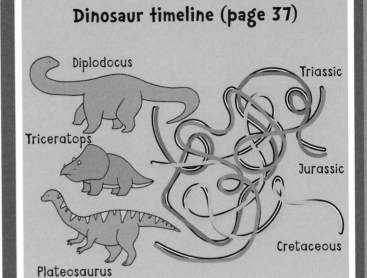

Diplodocus

Triassic

Triceratops

Jurassic

Cretaceous

Plateosaurus

Greedy dinosaur (page 37)

Shadow play (page 38)

Hide and seek (page 39)

There are 8 dinosaurs.

Make no bones about it (page 40)

Recycled letters (page 40)

FOSSIL
TRIASSIC
EXTINCT
JUNGLE
BONES
ROAR
JURASSIC
DIPLODOCUS

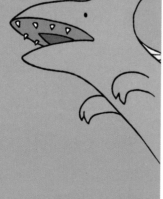

Hatch countdown (page 41)

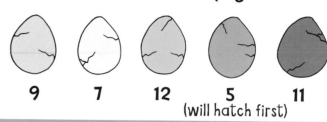

9   7   12   5   11

(will hatch first)

Spot the dinosaur (page 41)

30 spots

Baby dino nap time (page 43)

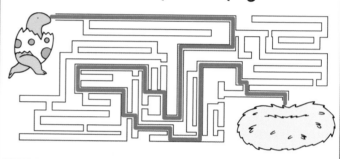

Weighty issues (page 43)

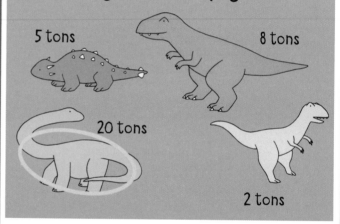

5 tons   8 tons

20 tons

2 tons

Chew it over (page 44)

Hidden dinosaurs (page 44)

```
P G B J U R A S S I C V K P
T R X H Q P K M Q X R X D Y
G B O N E S W P Z V E V Q P
H X S Y X T P V Y Q T Y X T
K F Q W S E G K J W A P T D
P O R X Z G T Y Q F C Q Y I
W S Z Q V O X C X W E D X P
Q S X D M S C Q V Z O X P L
R I V Q X A F V X Y U Z Q O
V L P V Q U X P Z S S A H D
Z Y X Q X R W Y X Z V Q L O
X G P Z Y U X P Q F X K X C
H Q X A X S W Z S P Y Q F U
D X G X Q Y K Q P W Z Q X S
```

Creepy crawlies (page 45)

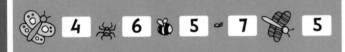

4   6   5   7   5

Big city giants (pages 46–47)

Funny bones (page 50)

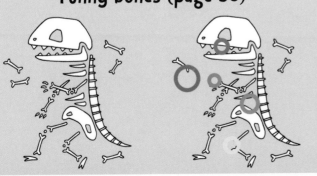

Flower power (page 50)

Muddled animals (page 53)

TURTLE
CROCODILE
BIRD
LIZARD
SNAKE
SHARK

Fossil race (page 53)

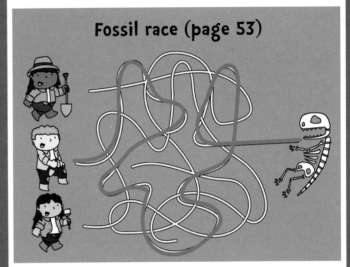

Colorful creatures (page 54)

Pink spots 4

Green tails 2

Yellow stripes 3

Blue spikes 2

Red legs 3

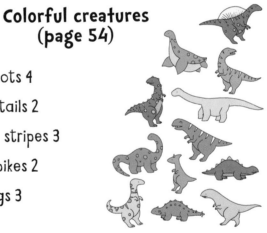

Gone missing (page 56)

First published 2018 by Button Books, an imprint of Guild of Master Craftsman Publications Ltd, Castle Place, 166 High Street, Lewes, East Sussex BN7 1XU, UK. Reprinted 2019. Text © GMC Publications Ltd, 2018. Copyright in the Work © GMC Publications Ltd, 2018. Illustrations © 2018 Jennifer Alliston. ISBN 978 1 78708 006 5. Distributed by Publishers Group West in the United States. All rights reserved. The right of Jennifer Alliston to be identified as the illustrator of this work has been asserted in accordance with the Copyright, Designs, and Patents Act 1988, sections 77 and 78. No part of this publication may be reproduced, stored in a retrieval system, or transmitted in any form or by any means without the prior permission of the publisher and copyright owner. While every effort has been made to obtain permission from the copyright holders for all material used in this book, the publishers will be pleased to hear from anyone who has not been appropriately acknowledged and to make the correction in future reprints. The publishers and author can accept no legal responsibility for any consequences arising from the application of information, advice or instructions given in this publication. A catalog record for this book is available from the British Library. Publisher: Jonathan Bailey. Production: Jim Bulley and Jo Pallett. Senior Project Editor: Wendy McAngus. Managing Art Editor: Gilda Pacitti. Color origination by GMC Reprographics. Printed and bound in China. Warning! Choking hazard—small parts. Not suitable for children under 3 years.